MORE AB

by

JAMES MARTIN

MORE ABOUT BOBBY

Typeset and printed by Thomson Litho Ltd, East Kilbride, Scotland

Contents

DEDICATION

Dedicated to our youngest grandchild, Ian Sommerville, who was not yet on the scene when my first Bobby book was published; and also to all those children of various churches who have listened to my Bobby stories.

Bobby is puzzled by the New Year

Bobby was very pleased and very excited when his Mum and Dad agreed to let him stay up to 'see the New Year in'. But he was a bit puzzled and also disappointed when the time came.

As the month of December drew near its end, Bobby heard Mum and Dad speak about the coming of the New Year. Dad said to Mum, 'I expect we'll be staying up as usual to see the New Year in. I'd better make sure we have something in the house to toast it with. Some of our friends will be calling in anyway to wish us a Happy New Year.'

'What's the New Year?' asked Bobby. Dad explained to him that when December came to an end, so did the present year. The first day of the next month, January, was the start of a brand new year. Grown-ups often waited up until midnight in order to give a welcome to the New Year.

'I would like to wait up and welcome it, too, when the time comes,' said Bobby.

'But that means waiting up until after midnight. You'll be far too tired.' That was Mum speaking.

'I could go to bed in the evening for a sleep and then get up again later. That way I wouldn't be too tired,' pleaded Bobby. So it was agreed that Bobby would be allowed to be up to welcome the New Year.

On the last day of December, Bobby went to bed early and slept soundly for a few hours. Soon after eleven o'clock Mum woke him up. He was rather sleepy-headed at first but by the time midnight approached he was wide awake. He was looking forward so much to seeing the New Year.

'What will happen when the New Year comes?' he asked.

'Whenever midnight comes,' Dad told him, 'I'll open the front door to let the New Year in and then we'll drink a toast to him.'

That is just what happened. As soon as the bells sounded on the television to announce midnight, Dad opened the front door for a minute. Then Mum gave Bobby a glass of lemonade and they all drank a toast of welcome to the New Year.

But Bobby was puzzled. He hadn't seen anyone come in through the door. 'Where is the New Year?' he asked, 'I can't see him.'

'Of course you can't,' said Dad. 'The New Year isn't a man. When we welcome the New Year, we welcome a new beginning, not a person. That

2 MORE ABOUT BOBBY

beginning is a time for asking God to help us be the best we can be during the year just starting. That's what welcoming the New Year is all about.'

After that Bobby felt he understood the New Year much better and he was glad he had been allowed to stay up to see it in.

Bobby has a 'Just a minute' phase

There was a time when Bobby was forever saying, 'Just a minute.' Nearly every time he was asked to do anything or called to go somewhere, that was the answer he was sure to give.

'Bobby,' Mum would call, 'come in for your dinner.'

'Just a minute,' Bobby would answer, and carry on doing whatever he was doing—usually for a number of minutes.

Or it might be, 'Bobby, will you give me a hand to lay the table?'

Again Mum would be sure to hear Bobby reply, 'Just a minute,' and by the time he appeared she would have the table laid.

It was the same on Sunday mornings when the family was going to church. Mum, Dad and Susan would be standing all ready to leave but Bobby would still be upstairs in his bedroom, busy about something or other.

'Bobby,' Mum would call, 'we're all ready to go. Come down at once.'

'Just a minute,' would come the response, but no Bobby would ever arrive downstairs until Dad shouted up loudly and sharply, 'BOBBY!'.

This became more and more of an annoyance to Mum and Dad. It often kept them late for this or for that. They made up their minds that something would have to be done to get Bobby to mend his ways. The very next day the opportunity came.

It was a Saturday and, since the sun was shining, they decided to go a run in the car to the seaside.

'That's what we'll do,' said Mum. 'Let's all get ready quickly. We'll leave in ten minutes time from now.'

Ten minutes later Mum, Dad and Susan were all ready to depart—but Bobby was still in his room. 'Come on, Bobby,' Mum called. 'It's time to go. Come at once.'

'Just a minute,' Bobby called back.

'Well,' said Mum, 'one minute and then we go whether you are here or not.'

A minute passed, then another minute—and still no Bobby.

'We're away, then,' Mum called up the stairs. All three of them rushed to the car, got in and drove away. Just as they drove off, Bobby came rushing out of the front door all upset but they pretended not to see him. Dad kept on driving, round the corner and out of Bobby's sight.

Once they were round the corner, Dad stopped the car. They waited a minute or two and then drove back to the house. They found Bobby in tears. He thought they had left him behind. He was so relieved to find that they had only been playing a trick on him.

But the trick worked. He stopped saying, 'Just a minute' and keeping everybody else back. He realised he had just been wasting other people's time and his own as well.

Jesus wants us to make the best possible use of our time, every minute of it.

Bobby discovers that size isn't everything

Bobby used to keep wishing that he was bigger. 'I'm so small,' he would say to himself. 'If only I was bigger, I would be able to do more and better things.'

Then one day he discovered that there were times when a small boy could be of more use than a grown man. This is what happened.

Mum noticed one evening a bit of a commotion around the house facing them on the other side of the street. This was occupied by Mr. and Mrs. Johnstone whose family had all grown up and left home. Mr. and Mrs. Johnstone were standing outside their house and both seemed very agitated.

Dad said, 'There must be something wrong. I'll go across and see if I can be of any help.'

Mum, Bobby and Susan watched from their front window as Dad went over. They saw him speaking to the Johnstones and then trying their front door. After that, all three walked round to the back of the house.

Before very long they appeared again at the front of the house. They talked together there for a few minutes and all of them looked worried. Then Dad's face brightened. He said something to the others before coming back across to his own house.

'Bobby,' he said, 'I think you can help. The Johnstones have locked themselves out and we can't find a way in. But there's a small window open at the back of the house. It's too small for me to get through it but I think you might be able to. Come and try.'

Bobby was thrilled to be asked to help in this way. Dad took him round to the back of the Johnstones' house and the open small window. With Mr. and Mrs. Johnstone looking on anxiously, Dad lifted Bobby up to the window. To everyone's delight Bobby was able to wriggle through. Next he climbed gently down to the floor on the other side. After that it was easy for him to open the front door and let the Johnstones in to their house.

Bobby was able to save the day because he was small. If he had been any bigger he wouldn't have been able to do it.

Boys and girls can sometimes help other people in ways that men and women aren't able to do. What is more, boys and girls have their own special service to give to Jesus.

Bobby buys grapes for his Gran

Bobby's Gran lives quite near. In fact Bobby can visit her by himself because he doesn't require to cross any main roads on the way.

He loves his Gran and she loves him. She is very kind to Bobby and to his little sister, Susan. One day Bobby had some money and he thought it would be a nice idea to use it to buy a present for his Gran. So he decided to get her a bunch of grapes.

He knew that she was very fond of grapes. As a matter of fact, so is Bobby. Perhaps he had it in the back of his mind that his Gran might share some of the grapes with him. But, as it turned out, she never got the chance. Oh, Bobby bought the grapes all right. But they never reached his Gran. This is why.

As Bobby left the fruit shop and began to walk along the road to his Gran's house, he suddenly started to worry. 'Gran likes sweet grapes. What if these grapes aren't sweet enough? I'd better try one just to make sure.' So he plucked a grape off the bunch and ate it.

'Yes,' he said to himself, 'that's fine. If they're all like that, Gran will enjoy them.' And then he thought, 'What if they're not all like that? I'd better try another one just to make sure.'

So Bobby plucked another grape from the bunch and ate it. He was pleased to find it was every bit as good as the first one. Then he began to worry again in case the rest of the grapes weren't as good as the first two. So he took another—and then another—and another.

By the time he reached his Gran's garden gate, there were only four grapes left. Bobby looked at the almost bare stalk and said to himself, 'I can hardly give Gran four grapes for a present. I'll just have to eat these four as well.' And he did.

Bobby started off with good intentions. He truly meant to give his Gran a lovely present. But on the way he gave in to the temptation to please himself instead of pleasing her.

It is very easy to be like Bobby at times and let selfishness stop us from carrying out a good intention. God is always pleased when we resist the temptation to be like that.

Bobby does some magic

Bobby can be very boastful at times. His Aunt Mary was not really surprised, therefore, when he was paying her a visit one day and suddenly said, 'I can do magic.'

'That's very nice,' said Aunt Mary. 'That's very clever of you.' But she didn't really think that a little boy like Bobby could do any proper magic. She thought he had probably been watching a magician on the television and was daydreaming about doing some magical tricks himself.

Bobby felt that Aunt Mary wasn't as impressed as she ought to have been, so he tried again. 'Aunt Mary, I really can do magic. I really can.'

'Can you, Bobby?' she replied. 'Tell me, then, what magic can you do?'

This was more like it. This was just what Bobby wanted to hear.

'I can put the whole of myself into a glass tumbler.'

'That is a bit much for me to believe, Bobby,' said Aunt Mary. 'How could you possibly do that?'

'Well, I can,' Bobby insisted. 'I can put the whole of myself into a glass tumbler. Wait and I'll show you. I'll go and get one of your tumblers and then you'll see.'

Off he went and returned with a glass tumbler in his hand. As Aunt Mary watched with great interest, he put it down on the table. Then he took a piece of paper. On it he printed, in big letters, MYSELF. Then he folded the paper and pushed it right inside the glass.

'There you are,' he shouted triumphantly. 'I have put the whole of MYSELF into your glass tumbler, haven't I?'

And so he had, the clever rascal. But it was a trick.

There's no trick, however, about the wonderful things Jesus says he can do to help us make the most of our lives. He really can do them.

Bobby and changes

One wet day, Mum gave Bobby and Susan a collection of family photographs to look through. She hoped this would keep them amused for a while.

It certainly did but it also caused Bobby a bit of disappointment about the way people and things can change so much.

To begin with, he and Susan were looking at their Mum and Dad's wedding pictures. They found them very, very interesting.

'Oh,' gasped Susan, 'doesn't Mum's wedding dress look lovely?'

'And doesn't Dad look very smart?,' said Bobby.

'They look so different, though, don't they, from what they are now?,' Susan said.

'Yes,' agreed Bobby, 'they do look a lot different. And so do the other people in the photographs, like Gran and Aunt Mary, for instance.'

They were so fascinated by the difference between how people looked in the photographs and how they looked now that they wanted to speak to Mum about it.

'Mum,' they called, 'please come for a minute.'

When she came, Bobby asked her, 'Why do you and Dad and the other people in the photographs look so different from what you really are?'

'Because,' laughed Mum, 'we do look different now from what we were then. A few years have passed since these photographs were taken and everybody changes with the passage of time. If you keep looking through these photographs, you'll see some of yourselves when you were younger and you'll see that you have changed, too.'

Sure enough, when they came to the photographs of themselves when younger, Bobby and Susan found that they looked quite a bit different from what they looked at the present time.

'Mum,' asked Bobby, 'does everybody change their appearance as they get older? Does nobody ever keep looking the same?'

'No, Bobby,' answered Mum. 'Everybody changes in appearance as the years pass.'

'Does that mean,' Bobby went on, 'that nobody ever stays the same?'

'Oh, yes,' said Mum. 'Jesus is always the same and always will be. The Bible tells us that and it's true.'

Bobby gets a shot at the pulpit microphone

Bobby's mum is one of the ladies who take it in turn to arrange the flowers for the Sunday services in their church. When it is her turn, Bobby likes to go with her. He enjoys being in the church when it's empty. He likes walking round. He likes sitting in the pew and pretending to be listening to the minister in the pulpit.

He would have liked to go up into the pulpit, too, and pretend he was preaching the sermon. But Mum would never let him go there. She said only the minister could give him permission to do that.

Well, one day when Mum was doing the church flowers and Bobby was with her, the minister came into the church. He chatted to them both and seemed pleased that Bobby was interested in the church building. This gave Bobby the confidence to make a request.

'Please, sir,' he said, 'would it be all right if I went up into the pulpit? I've often seen you there and I would like to see what it's like.'

'Of course, Bobby,' the minister replied. 'Up you go.'

Bobby didn't hesitate. In no time at all he had climbed the pulpit steps. He stood there looking down towards the seat he sat in on Sundays. 'I'll pretend I'm the minister taking the Sunday service,' he said to himself. 'I'll preach a sermon to my mum as she sorts the flowers. I'll speak into the microphone like the minister does. When my voice booms out, Mum will get a big surprise.'

He stepped across to the microphone and started his sermon. 'Mums should always be kind to their little boys and give them plenty of chocolate biscuits.' Bobby thought his mum would be sure to look up when his voice boomed out through the microphone but she just keep on working away.

In fact, Mum didn't even hear him. For his voice didn't boom out after all. The microphone, you see, wasn't switched on. The minister, however, noticed what was happening and switched it on. Then Bobby's voice did boom out and he was very pleased.

The microphone needed to be switched on before it could work. It's much the same with Christian faith. We have to switch it on before it can help us.

Bobby gives Uncle Jim a present

Bobby is very fond of his Uncle Jim. That's why he wanted to give him a really special present for his birthday. So he looked around for something that no one else was likely to give him, although he knew it would have to be quite cheap since he didn't have very much money.

One day he saw in a shop window what he thought would be the very thing. Bobby had never seen anything like it before and he was sure Uncle Jim did not have one. It was a giant comb. It must have been ten times the size of an ordinary comb and, what's more, it wasn't very expensive. Bobby had enough money in his pocket so he just went in and bought it right away.

He did not tell anyone what he had bought for Uncle Jim's birthday. He wanted it to be a complete surprise. He wrapped it up in coloured paper and on Uncle Jim's birthday he took it along and handed it to him, saying, 'Many happy returns, Uncle Jim. Here's a birthday present for you.'

Uncle Jim said, 'Thank your very much, Bobby. It is very kind of you to remember your uncle's birthday like this.' He was very pleased at getting a birthday present from Bobby and he wondered what it could be.

'It's a very special present,' Bobby said. 'I don't think anybody in the whole world will ever have been given a birthday present like this. Open it up and see what it is.'

Uncle Jim opened the parcel there and then. What a surprise he got. He hadn't expected anything like that. 'Thank you very much, Bobby,' he said. 'It's a lovely present and you've been very kind.'

Uncle Jim WAS pleased but he was also a little bit disappointed for the giant comb was too big to be of any use to him. It was probably all right for combing a giant's hair but it was much too large to deal with Uncle Jim's. It was actually quite an unsuitable present to give.

That was a great pity because whenever we give a present to anyone we should try to give something suitable that will be of use to whoever it is. Unsuitable presents can be such a waste.

That's what makes it so wonderful that at the first Christmas God gave the world a present that was suitable for everyone. He gave us Jesus to be the friend of all.

Bobby falls out with Jimmy

Like most boys and girls Bobby has a best friend. His best friend's name is Jimmy and they get on very well together. They see each other nearly every day. When school is on they usually play together for an hour or two after school, and they always meet with each other on Saturday mornings.

Now and again, however, they have a disagreement. This is the sort of thing that can happen with the best of friends. Usually when Bobby and Jimmy have a disagreement it doesn't amount to very much. But there was one occasion which seemed to be very serious.

I don't know what it was all about but they fell out rather badly. Bobby was really angry with Jimmy whatever it was. He felt so upset that he wrote a letter to Jimmy telling him so. This is what he wrote: 'Dear Jimmy, I am very annoyed with you. I don't want anything to do with you again for I am really very angry with you. Signed, Bobby.

PS. I'll be round for you at the usual time on Saturday.'

Bobby was upset with Jimmy but at the same time he had the good sense not to stop being friends with him because of it, whatever it was. I'm glad to say that when the Saturday morning came, Bobby did go round for Jimmy and they have continued to be the best of friends. Bobby in fact had already stopped being angry by that time. As a matter of fact he had forgotten what it was all about anyway.

Sometimes people fall out with friends over something or other. Sometimes they stop being friends any more because of it. It is very sad when that happens because good friends are so important to have.

Thank goodness God never gives us up even when we let him down. There are times when he is displeased with some of the things we do or fail to do. But he keeps on loving us just the same and keeps on wanting us to be his friends and followers.

Bobby refuses to be a 'Sunbeam for Jesus'

In Bobby's Sunday School they sometimes have a period of singing choruses. Bobby loves these sessions. So do all the other children. They sing the choruses as loudly as they can,

Bobby's special favourite is 'Wide, wide as the ocean'. Here is how it goes:

> 'Wide, wide as the ocean,
> High as the heavens above,
> Deep, deep as the deepest sea,
> Is my Father's love'.

He is very fond of a great many others as well. Like 'I'm H-A-P-P-Y' and 'Climb, climb up sunshine mountain'.

One day they sang 'Jesus wants me for a sunbeam'. Bobby and the others enjoyed singing that one, too. When they had finished singing it, the leader of their Sunday School department said to the boys and girls, 'Jesus would like you all to be sunbeams for him. How many of you would like to be a sunbeam for Jesus? Put up your hands if you would.'

They all put up their hands—except Bobby. The leader was surprised that Bobby didn't put up his hand. 'Bobby,' he said, 'I thought you would want to be a sunbeam for Jesus.'

'So I would,' Bobby replied, 'but I can't today because my mum told me I had to hurry home from Sunday School as we're going out to visit my aunt.'

Poor Bobby. He thought being a sunbeam for Jesus would keep him back from being home on time. He didn't realise that Jesus wants us to be sunbeams for him just where we are—not just in church but also at home and school and play. He wants us for his sake to shed light and joy into the lives of other people.

Bobby hides from the thunder and lightning

Do you know anyone who likes thunder and lightning? I don't. But I know lots of people who find it very frightening. When the thunder rolls and the lightning flashes some people hide themselves away in the darkest corner they can find. If possible they like some hidey-hole where they can neither hear the thunder nor see the lightning.

Bobby is like that. What he usually does when the thunder and lightning start is to rush upstairs to his bedroom. When he gets there he dives into his bed and pulls the bedclothes right over his head.

One day, when a storm broke and the thunder started, Bobby leaped off his chair and rushed out of the room. Mum knew that he was heading for his bedroom. What she didn't know was that he never got there. Just as he got to the foot of the stairs, the thunder gave the loudest peal Bobby had ever heard in his life. It gave him a terrible fright. He was so scared that he didn't take time to go up the stairs. He simply rushed into the big cupboard they had at the foot of the stairs, pulled the door shut, closed his eyes tight and put his fingers in his ears.

The storm actually lasted only a very short time. It was all over in a few minutes and then the sun came out to make a beautiful day. But Bobby knew nothing about that. He was still in the cupboard, hearing and seeing nothing. And at first no one came to tell him. Mum thought he was in his bedroom and thought he had just stayed there to play once the thunder and lightning stopped. It was only after a time she began to think to herself, 'Bobby's very quiet up there. I wonder if he's fallen asleep. I'd better go and see.'

Upstairs she went—but, of course, Bobby wasn't there. Down she came again and called out as loudly as she could, 'Bobby, where are you?' It was lucky that she was standing just beside the cupboard door when she did this, otherwise Bobby might not have heard her. But he did hear her and out he came.

When he saw the sunshine, he said, 'Oh, what a lovely day it is now.' 'Yes,' said his Mum, 'and it's been like this for the past half hour. You would have been better outside playing than shut up in that stuffy cupboard.'

'So I would,' Bobby agreed. 'I've missed myself, haven't I, because I was afraid of the thunder?'

He did indeed; and sometimes people miss out on good things in life because they are afraid of bad things. Jesus tells us that if we put our trust in him we needn't be afraid of anything because even in the worst of times he will be there to give us comfort and strength.

Bobby washes his face in the May Dew

Bobby was out of his bed very early on the first day of May. It was a lovely, sunny morning and Bobby was outside in the garden before anyone else in the house was up. The reason was that he wanted to wash his face in the May Dew.

It was his best friend, Jimmy, who was the cause of it. One day, near the end of April, Jimmy said to Bobby, 'Have you heard about the May Dew, Bobby?'

'No, I haven't,' answered Bobby. 'What is it?'

'Dew,' said Jimmy, 'is something that comes down on to the grass on dry nights in the summer time and leaves it wet in the morning. On the morning of the first of May the dew is supposed to be special. If you get up early and wash your face in it, they say it will make you very handsome.'

'Is that really true?' asked Bobby in amazement.

'I don't know for sure,' replied Jimmy, 'but that's what they say.'

'It sounds good,' Bobby said. 'I think I'll try it for myself.'

And so he did. That's why if you'd been standing outside Bobby's house early on the first of May you would have seen him coming out of the house and going on to the lawn to wash his face in the dew.

I can tell you, however, that Bobby felt very let down. He rushed back into the house and went at once to the mirror to look at his face. He hoped it would have become more handsome. But it was just the same as it had been before.

'Perhaps,' he thought to himself, 'perhaps it doesn't work right away. Maybe I'll notice a difference tomorrow.' But there was no difference the next day. Nor the next. In fact washing his face in the May Dew made not the slightest difference to Bobby's looks.

Bobby came to realise that the story about the May Dew was only a story; and he has decided never to bother again to get up early to wash his face in it.

This makes it all the more wonderful that the Bible stories of what Jesus can do for us are not just empty stories but true ones. He really can forgive our sins. He really can help us to live life well and bravely. He really can give us life at its best.

Bobby learns about St. Swithin

Everybody in the district where Bobby lived was heartily sick of the wet weather. It had been pouring for days on end and they had all had quite enough of it, including Bobby. But he still had his sense of humour and the bad weather led him to think up a trick to play on his father.

'Dad,' he said, 'I know a bad word of four letters. Can you guess what it is?'

Dad was taken aback and looked at Bobby very suspiciously. He wondered what was coming. 'No,' he said cautiously. 'I can't guess what it is. Give me a clue.'

'All right,' Bobby replied, 'here's your clue. Everybody is talking about this and it makes everybody use an umbrella.' Dad's face lit up at once and he smiled. Now he knew what the word was. 'The word is ''rain'',' he said; and he was right.

Then Dad went on to say something else which surprised Bobby. 'I know a little poem about rain. Here it is:

> If it should rain on St. Swithin's Day,
> The rain will stay and stay and stay.
> For forty days you'll need your wellies
> Or sit inside and watch your tellies.'

'That's very good,' said Bobby, 'but what's St. Swithin's Day?'

'July 15 is St. Swithin's Day,' Dad told him. 'And there's a legend which says if it rains on that day, it will rain for the next 40 days; but if it's dry on that day, it will be dry on the next 40.'

That is the legend and some people believe it. You will find them anxiously studying the sky on July 15. They think it will tell them what the weather is going to be like for the next 40 days. But the legend is not true. You can't depend on it to work out.

One thing we can all depend on is the word of Jesus. His promises can be trusted completely.

Bobby examines the back of Mrs. Thomson's head

Bobby's mum was having a visitor for tea. Mrs. Thomson was her name. She was a good friend of Bobby's mum but she was a person who noticed everthing. As a result Mum was anxious that everything in the house would be just right when Mrs. Thomson came.

She spent ever so much time cleaning and tidying. While she was doing it, she said to Bobby, 'Make sure that all your toys and things are put away tidily before Mrs. Thomson comes. I want everything spick and span for her coming. If there's anything not as it should be, she'll notice it. She's got eyes in the back of her head.'

When Mrs. Thomson arrived, she was given the best chair to sit in and Mum and she began to have a real good chat. While this was going on Bobby kept wandering round behind Mrs. Thomson's chair and staring at her from the back. At last his mum said, 'What are you playing at, Bobby? It's very rude to stand behind our visitor the way you're doing.'

What a shock Mum got when Bobby said, 'I'm just wanting to see the eyes you said Mrs. Thomson has in the back of her head. I've been looking and looking and I can't see them.'

Mum, of course, hadn't meant that Mrs. Thomson had actual eyes in the back of her head. She was using what we call a figure of speech and she meant that Mrs. Thomson was a very noticing kind of person. Mum was very embarrassed when Bobby said what he did. Fortunately, Mrs. Thomson has a good sense of humour. She thought it was a great joke and laughed heartily.

It is more than just a figure of speech to say that God sees everything. For he really does. He knows everything we do. He sees us at our worst as well as at out best. The marvellous thing is that he keeps loving us just the same.

Bobby and the Camelephantelopelicanary

Bobby was being very, very cross one day and it was all because he was in a discontented mood. 'Why can't I run faster?' he said crossly. 'I wish I was like Jack Smith. He can run faster than I can.'

He was just as cross the next day and that was because he was discontented about something else. A new boy with bright red hair had come into Bobby's school class. Bobby was full of admiration for the new boy's red hair and wished that he had red hair, too.

He complained to his mum, 'Why couldn't I have been born with red hair? That's what I'd like to have had.'

'It doesn't do any good to wish for something you can't possibly have,' Mum said. 'We've all to make the best of what we are. Let me tell you about the discontented camel.' Bobby thought this sounded interesting and he settled down to listen.

There was a camel once—this was the story Mum told Bobby—who was very discontented with being a camel. One day he made friends with a magician. He told his new friend how unhappy he was at just being a camel.

'Well, then,' said the magician, 'I will help you. Whenever we meet another animal that has some feature you would like, I'll work my magic and let you have it.'

That will be great, thought the camel, and off they set together. The first animal they met was an elephant and the camel said, 'I wish I had a trunk like that elephant so that I could pick up things from the ground.'

No sooner had he said it than he found he had a trunk just like the elephant had. The magician said, 'You're no longer just a camel. Now you're a camelephant.'

The camelephant was happy but only for a moment. For he caught sight of an antelope racing past like the wind. 'Oh,' he said, 'I wish I had legs like that antelope so that I could run like him.' At once he had antelope legs and the magician said, 'Now you are a camelephantelope.'

For a short time again the camelephantelope was happy but then he saw a pelican carrying a large amount of fish in its mouth. 'I wish I had a large mouth like that so that I could carry a lot of food about with me.'

At once he had a pelican's mouth and the magician said, 'You have now become a camelephantelopelican.' Again the camelephantelopelican was happy but only for a short time. His happiness lasted only until a canary flew past singing in the lovely way that canaries sing. 'Oh,' said the camelephantelopelican, 'how I wish I could sing like that canary.' The very next instant he had a canary's voice and the magician said to him, 'You are now a camelephantelopelicanary.'

Again he was happy and contented—but once more only for a minute or two. For they met a crowd of animals and people who began to laugh and make fun of him when they saw him. 'Look at this funny creature,' they said. 'How ugly he is with his bits and pieces of other creatures.'

The camelephantelopelicanary realised then that he had been much better off when he was the camel that God had meant him to be.

'I've been very foolish,' he said to the magician. 'Please make me a camel again.'

His friend said, 'I think you are being very wise. You were much better off the way you were.' At once he was back to being a camel and he never again wished that he was somebody else. He just tried to be the best kind of camel he could.

Bobby enjoyed hearing that story and he thinks of it every time he begins to feel discontented.

Bobby discovers the meaning of 'Robert'

Bobby isn't the name that is on his birth certificate. Bobby is just a shortened form of Robert and that is his proper name.

Bobby always knew that his proper name was Robert, although no one ever calls him that except his school teacher. Everyone else calls him Bobby and that's what he likes to be called.

At the same time he is proud of his proper name, too, especially since he found out what Robert means. One day at school teacher was telling the class that lots of proper names had a meaning and she told him that Robert meant 'bright' or 'happy'.

Bobby was very pleased to know this. On the way home from school he met the minister and was so full of his new discovery that he had to tell him.

'Do you know,' he said, 'that my name, Robert, means bright or happy? Isn't that good?'

'That's very good,' said the minister, 'and it suits you. I hope you will always live up to it.'

'I will do my best,' Bobby replied. 'What is your first name? Do you try to live up to it?'

The minister laughed. 'My first name is James,' he said, 'and that doesn't have as nice a meaning as your name has. James really means ''usurper''. It is really the same name as Jacob in the Old Testament who pushed out his brother Esau from his rightful place and took it himself. But it can also be taken to mean one who is ready to take the place of someone who is in need of help. That's how I prefer to think of it. It's always best to try to live up to the best that your name means.'

'What about the name of Jesus?' Bobby asked. 'Did he live up to his name?' The minister was a little surprised to hear Bobby ask such a serious question. But he was pleased, too, especially since he was able to answer it.

'He certainly did,' the minister said to Bobby. 'The name Jesus means ''Saviour'' or ''Rescuer'' and Jesus is able to rescue his followers from sin and lead them into eternal life.'

Bobby does some juggling

Bobby and the minister get along famously together and they sometimes have friendly competitions with each other. For instance, each is for ever trying to give the other a harder riddle or trying to tell a funnier joke or trying to catch him out with a trick. Sometimes Bobby thinks he has won the contest but sometimes he has to admit that the minister has given a better riddle or told a funnier joke or come up with a better trick.

When this happens, Bobby doesn't enjoy having to own up to being beaten. One day, however, he had no choice. The minister said, 'Bobby, I have learned to do something that you can't do. I have learned to juggle a bit and I can keep four balls in the air at the same time. Look, I'll show you.'

He took four balls from his pocket and began to juggle them from hand to hand. Sure enough he was able to keep them all in the air at once without letting any of them fall to the ground.

'Perhaps if you practice hard enough, Bobby,' the minister said, 'you'll be able to match me the next time I see you.'

'Just you wait and see,' Bobby replied. 'When you come back round, I'll do better than you. I'll keep FIVE balls in the air at once.'

After the minister had gone away, Bobby gathered up some balls and began to try to juggle them. But he found it very difficult. The balls kept falling to the ground. It looked as if he would never be able to keep his promise.

All the same, the next time the minister called in, Bobby didn't seem at all dismayed when he was asked, 'Well, Bobby, how's your juggling getting on?' In fact he looked quite smug and to the minister's surprise, he said, 'Fine. You kept four balls in the air at once but I can keep five balls in the air.'

The minister laughed. 'I find that hard to believe, Bobby. In fact I won't believe it until I see it for myself.'

'I'll show you, then,' said Bobby and went away and collected five balls. But he didn't attempt to juggle them. He had brought along a large paper bag as well. He put the five balls into it and held the bag up as high as he could. 'See, there,' he yelled with glee, 'I'm keeping five balls in the air all at the same time.'

So he was, but not by juggling them. It was a trick. The glorious thing about the promises Jesus makes is that he is able to keep them without any trickery.

Bobby discovers that soup tastes good

The first time Bobby was given soup as part of his meal was when he was still a very small boy. He wasn't very sure of this new item of food and, unfortunately, Mum hadn't cooled it down quite enough. As soon as he took the first spoonful, he let out a yell and spat it out. 'That's terrible stuff,' he yelled. 'It burns. I hate it, I hate it.'

After that Mum just couldn't get him to take soup. She tried coaxing him. She tried ordering him. But it was no use. Bobby simply refused to take soup, no matter what kind it was. 'I hate soup. I hate soup.' He kept saying, 'I'm sure it would just make me sick if I took it.'

Then one day something happened that changed things. He was invited to a birthday party. It was actually his favourite girl friend's birthday party and it was in her house. Bobby was delighted to be going to the party. He was quite excited, too, for he was fond of Margaret and he was anxious to make a good impression.

It was a cold day and when they all sat down at the table for the birthday meal, there was a shock for Bobby. Margaret's mother said, 'Since it's a cold day, I thought it would be a good idea to give you a bowl of soup to start with. I hope you enjoy it.'

Bobby didn't know what to do. 'What if I say that I don't like soup and refuse to take it?' he was thinking. 'Margaret might think me terrible and stop liking me because of it. I'd better just take it but I hope it doesn't make me sick.'

He took the soup and it didn't make kim sick. In fact, to his surprise he found that he liked it very much. He liked it so much that he had a second helping.

Bobby never refuses soup now. As a matter of fact, it's one of his favourite dishes. He used to be so sure that he hated it but that was before he had given it a trial. Once he tried it, he discovered that it tasted good and realised how much he had been missing in not taking it before.

Sometimes people are like that with following Jesus. Before they give it a trial, they convince themselves they won't like it. When they do give it a trial they find out how wrong they were. Following Jesus can be the best of fun.

Bobby plays at churches with Susan

Away from his own home and garden, Bobby would never dream of playing with his little sister, Susan. He is too frightened that any of his school chums might see him. He knows that they would tease him for playing with a girl, even though she is his sister.

It's a different story, though, when he's at home and has no one else to play with. One of the games he and Susan like to play is 'churches'. They both go regularly to church and Sunday School and they enjoy pretending to conduct a church service.

Bobby, I am afraid, usually insists, since he is older than Susan, that he plays the part of the minister. He is the one who usually takes the pulpit, says the prayers, reads the lessons and preaches the sermon. Susan nearly every time has to be content with being the congregation.

All the same, Bobby doesn't get it all his own way. Even when he is the 'minister', Susan often argues with him and sometimes she just goes her own way.

That happened one time when they had a disagreement about what hymn to sing next. Bobby announced, 'Now we will sing, ''If I come to Jesus'', because that's my favourite.' But Susan said, 'I want to sing ''Jesus loves me'', because that's MY favourite.'

Bobby wasn't pleased. 'You'll have to sing what I say we're going to sing.'

'No, I won't,' said Susan. 'I'll sing what I like.'

Bobby thought that if he started singing his hymn Susan would have to join in. So he began to sing, 'If I come to Jesus' at the top of his voice. But Susan was determined not to give in. So she started to sing at the top of HER voice 'Jesus loves me'.

It sounded awful and Mum came rushing in from the next room. 'What's all this about?' she said. 'Why are you making such a terrible row?'

'We're singing our favourite hymn,' Bobby and Susan said, both speaking at once.

'Well, it doesn't sound like a hymn to me,' said Mum. 'It sounds more like a cat whose tail has been trodden on and that's because you're each singing something different. How about taking your favourite hymns one at a time and both of you singing the same thing together?'

They did what Mum suggested and what a difference it made. 'That's MUCH better,' Mum said. 'Your singing is much more pleasant to listen to now. Do you know, Bobby, that's almost a sermon for you without needing to preach. God doesn't expect us all to agree about everything but he does want us to live in harmony together.'

Bobby and his Dad's toothpaste

What Bobby likes best about cleaning his teeth is the fun he gets squeezing the toothpaste out of the tube. That's what got him into bother with his Dad one day.

It was the day Bobby went into the bathroom and discovered that his Dad had a brand new tube of toothpaste lying there. Bobby thought it looked splendid. He picked it up to look at it and he said to himself, 'What fun it would be to squeeze some of the paste out of this lovely new tube. But it would be naughty to do that and Dad would be angry. I'd better not.'

Bobby didn't put the toothpaste down, however. He kept it in his hand and kept looking at it. He kept thinking how much he was sure to enjoy squeezing it. Then he said to himself, 'If I just squeezed out a very little, Dad might never notice. I think I'll just do that.'

Before he could change his mind, Bobby let his fingers squeeze the tube. But he pressed harder than he meant to do and it was quite a lot of toothpaste that came out.

'Oh, dear,' Bobby groaned. 'Dad is bound to notice that amount of toothpaste missing. What will I do?'

He thought for a moment with a very worried frown. Then his face cleared. 'I know what I'll do,' he said. 'I'll push the toothpaste back into the tube and Dad will never know I've touched it.'

He set to work right away. He pushed and pushed but he found it quite impossible to get any of the paste back in. All he succeeded in doing was to squeeze more paste out with his efforts. What a mess there was. The toothpaste was all over the wash-hand basin and all over Bobby himself.

He made up his mind that there was nothing else for it but to own up to his Dad and tell him what he had done. So he went to Dad, thinking to himself, 'I'll just have to take what I get for being naughty.'

'Dad,' he said, 'I'm very sorry but I've squeezed some of the tooth-paste out of your new tube and made a bit of a mess.'

'I'd better come and see just what you've done,' Dad said. Bobby went with him, sure that he was in for a big row once Dad saw the mess. Instead he was in for a surprise. 'You've certainly been naughty, Bobby, and I'm not pleased with you because of it. However, you've owned up and you've said you were sorry, so we'll say no more about it. But don't do anything like that again.'

And, do you know, that's just how God deals with us if we admit our faults to him and say we're sorry.

Bobby's minister is absent-minded

Bobby had a good laugh when his minister was absent-minded in Bobby's house.

The minister had come to visit. Mum, Dad, Bobby and Susan all enjoyed the visit very much for the minister always was easy to talk to. After a while the minister said, 'I've enjoyed my visit but I'll need to go now as I've other visits to make.'

He rose to his feet and prepared to leave. As Bobby's dad opened the door for him, the minister took his hat from the hallstand where he'd left it and put it on his head. Just then Mum remembered something else she wanted to say to him and started to speak.

This extra conversation lasted a minute or two and when it was over, the minister said, 'Well, I must go this time.' Then he looked around and said, 'Now, where did I put my hat? I know I had it when I came in.'

Bobby was almost helpless with laughter at this because, of course, the hat was still on the minister's head where he had put it just a short time ago. He had absent-mindedly forgotten that and Bobby thought it was so terribly funny that he laughed and laughed.

The minister laughed, too, when Bobby spluttered through his laughter, 'It's on your head, minister, it's on your head.'

'So it is,' he said. 'So it is. That was very absent-minded of me, wasn't it?'

Bobby was laughing then but he wasn't laughing so much a day or two later. And that was to do with a hat as well.

He was at the birthday party of a boy who stayed just along the street from Bobby. The party was in the boy's house and during it the children all put on funny paper hats. When the time came to go home, Bobby completely forgot that he was wearing his funny hat. As a result, he walked along the street with it still on his head.

He couldn't understand why everybody was turning to look at him and laughing as he passed by. It was only when he reached home and Mum said, 'Bobby, why were you wearing that silly hat coming along the street?' that he realised what he had done. He felt quite cross with himself for being absent-minded.

Most people are absent-minded at times.

But God never is. He never forgets about any of us.

Bobby visits the Old Folks' Home

Bobby's minister conducts a short church service on Sunday afternoons in a home for old people. They have a little organ to help with the singing. Bobby's mum goes along sometimes to play the organ.

One day she took Bobby with her. He was pleased to go and he was quite a help to the minister. He handed out the hymn books to the men and women who had gathered in the common room for the service. He joined in the singing because the hymns were ones that he knew. And when the service was over he collected in the hymn books again.

While the minister and his mum were tidying up and putting things away, Bobby went round speaking to the old people. He enjoyed that, too. He had a very interesting conversation with one old man.

'It's a real bad day, isn't it?' said Bobby to start the conversation, because the rain was simply pouring down outside. To Bobby's great surprise the old man replied, 'Oh, no, it's not. It's a GOOD day. Every day is a good day.'

'How can you say it's a good day?' Bobby protested. 'Look at the rain.'

'Yes,' the old man said, 'but, you see, it's not raining everywhere. The sun is always shining somewhere, and, even when it is raining, God still loves us. We ought to remember that whenever the weather is bad around us.'

Bobby was very impressed. 'I will, sir,' he said. 'Whenever we have a rainy day, I'll try to remember how you told me that the sun is sure to be shining somewhere.'

'That's good,' said his new friend, 'and if you do that you'll understand why my favourite hymn chorus is:

> Count your blessings, name them one by one,
> Count your blessings, see what God has done.
> Count your blessings, name them one by one,
> And it will surprise you what the Lord has done.'

Bobby's new friend certainly gave him something to think about on the way home that day.

Bobby races at the Sunday School outing

The first time Bobby was at the Sunday School outing he enjoyed it very much—except for the races. He enjoyed the journey in the bus with the other children, the teachers and quite a lot of parents. He enjoyed it all the more because it was a lovely sunny day. He enjoyed the picnic food and he enjoyed the games.

But he didn't enjoy the races because he came last in every one. The trouble was that although he ran fast, he never managed to run straight. He was so interested in everything else that was happening and all the people looking on that he kept looking around him as he ran. The result was that he kept straying all over the place as he ran. Everyone else in the race ran straight for the tape. Although Bobby could run faster than they could, they all finished before him.

The next time the Sunday School outing came round, Bobby said, 'I don't think I want to go this time.'

'Why not?' asked his Dad. 'I thought you enjoyed it the last time.'

'I did enjoy it,' said Bobby, 'except for the races. I didn't enjoy them because I was last every time.'

'I know why you were last,' said Dad. 'It was because you ran from side to side. If you run straight for the finishing line, you'll do much better.'

'No,' Bobby said. 'I don't think I want to go. I would likely find myself running all over the place again and coming in last. I wouldn't like that.'

'I'll tell you what,' said Dad. 'I'll stand behind the finishing line. If you keep your eyes on me and run towards me that will keep you on the straight line of the race.'

Bobby wasn't very sure of this at first but the more he thought about it the more he thought it might be worth trying. He decided to go to the outing after all and he decided to follow his Dad's suggestion in the races.

Dad's idea worked. Dad took up a position behind the finishing line where Bobby could see him clearly. Bobby fixed his eyes on Dad and ran straight towards him as fast as he could. What a difference it made. Instead of coming in last, he came in first.

The Bible tells us that the best way to run the race of life is to keep our eyes fixed on Jesus.

Bobby tells Susan about the Robin Redbreast

Bobby and his little sister, Susan, like to watch the birds that visit their garden and love to hear them singing. All kinds of birds come into their garden, magpies and finches, starlings and blue tits, sparrows, thrushes and blackbirds—and a whole lot more.

Bobby and Susan love to see them strutting about on the lawn and digging for worms with their beaks. Most of all they love to see them taking a bath in the bird bath which stands in the garden and which Dad always keeps filled to the brim.

One day a robin redbreast came into the garden and he seemed to take up residence there. Every day after that whenever they went into the garden they were sure to see him hopping here and hopping there. They grew very fond of him and he seemed to be fond of them, too. At any rate he never flew away when they came near. He just kept hopping around, watching them all the time with his beady eyes.

At school one day soon after the robin came, Bobby's teacher told his class a story about how the robin got his red breast. Bobby was fascinated by the story and could hardly wait for school to be over so that he could rush home to tell it to Susan.

This was the story.

On the day that Jesus was crucified, the Roman soldiers made a crown of thorns and pressed it on his head. They pressed it down so hard that the thorns pierced his skin and caused the blood to flow down his face. The robin (who didn't have a red breast then) was flying past just at that moment. He was sad to see Jesus suffering such pain and wished he could do something to help. So he flew up and with his little beak began to pluck some of the thorns out of Jesus' brow. As he did this a drop of Jesus' blood fell on his breast and stained it red. According to the story, the robin has had a red breast ever since.

This is a kind of story that is called a legend. That is to say, it may not actually have happened but it has a lesson to teach us just the same. The reason that we often see a robin redbreast on a Christmas card is to remind us of this. The baby born in Bethlehem on the first Christmas Day grew up to die on Calvary's Cross so that he could become our Saviour and Friend.

Bobby in the Nativity Play

Bobby came home from school one day all excited. 'Mum, Mum,' he called out before he was properly through the front door, 'I've got a part in the nativity play at the school.'

'That's wonderful,' said Mum. 'I'm so pleased. What part have you got?'

'I'm not allowed to tell you,' Bobby replied. 'It's all to be kept a secret until the day so that it will be a surprise to the parents when they come to see the play. But teacher said my part was a very important one.'

Mum was nearly as excited as Bobby and so was Dad when he heard about it. They were so pleased for Bobby and they wondered what his part might be. It would hardly be that of Joseph, they thought, but perhaps it might be a Wise Man or a shepherd—or even the innkeeper.

The play was being staged in the school's assembly hall and a large crowd of parents came along to see it. Bobby's Mum and Dad were among them. They still did not know what part he was playing for he had kept it a secret as his teacher had told him to. Wondering what it would be added to their excitement.

The nativity play went very well and was a great success. But Bobby's Mum and Dad got a big surprise when they found out what his part was. He wasn't Joseph and he wasn't a Wise Man and he wasn't a shepherd and he wasn't the innkeeper. Bobby didn't even have one word to say in the play. Bobby was a BUSH. Mum and Dad were a wee bit disappointed but they were very proud of Bobby all the same. He did his part so well. He stood there on the stage holding a large bunch of holly above his head and he stood perfectly still all through the play just as he was supposed to do.

Bobby's part in the play was one of the small parts but it WAS important just as his teacher had said. It mattered very much that Bobby should do it well.

Not everyone can have a big part in a play but the smaller parts are important, too. It is like that with life also. Some people get smaller parts to play than others do but they all matter. God wants us to do our best whether we have a large part or a small one and Jesus is always willing to help us do that.

Bobby and birthday cards

Bobby likes birthdays, especially his own.

He is always very interested when he learns of someone having a birthday. He's even more interested when it is someone he knows well. If it is one of his friends, that's better still. If that friend is having a birthday party and invites Bobby to it, that makes it just wonderful.

Oh, yes, Bobby likes other people's birthdays, that's for sure. But most of all he likes it when it is his own birthday. And one of the things he likes best about his own birthday is getting birthday cards through the post. He is so excited and thrilled when the postman comes and pops through the letter-box cards that are addressed to him.

He was telling me about this one day and about how good it was to get birthday cards through the post. I asked him, 'Why is it, Bobby, that you like getting birthday cards so much?' 'I like it 'he said,' because every card I get means that someone has remembered me.'

It's always good to be remembered, whether we are young or old, and whether it is with a birthday card or a present or simply a kind word or a kind look.

The opposite truth is that it's a terrible thing to be forgotten—or even to think that we are forgotten. There was one awful day when Bobby thought that his Dad had forgotten him. Dad always comes to the church hall to collect him and take him home after the Anchor Boys but one night when the meeting was over Dad wasn't there.

The officer-in-charge said, 'Don't worry, Bobby. I'll wait with you until your Dad comes. He'll likely be here in a minute.'

But Dad didn't come in a minute. As the time kept passing and Dad still hadn't appeared, Bobby's heart sank lower and lower. He was sure his Dad had forgotten him and that made him very sad.

Then Dad arrived. 'I'm very sorry, Bobby,' he said. 'When I came out to the car I found it had a flat tyre. I had to change the wheel. That's why I'm late.'

'I'm so glad to see you, Dad,' Bobby said. 'I thought you had forgotten me.'

'Of course I hadn't forgotten you,' said Dad. 'How could I forget you when I love you?'

We can all be sure of this, that God will never forget us. He loves us so much.

Bobby doesn't hear Mum

Bobby is quite a good boy most of the time—but not all of the time.

Bobby is quite an obedient boy most of the time—but not all of the time.

Sometimes when Bobby doesn't want to do something that Mum wants him to do, he pretends not to hear her. Sometimes he behaves as if he were a bit deaf.

That was how it was one day when Mum called to him as he was out in the garden playing by himself and having a very good time. He didn't want to interrupt his game. When Mum came to the door and called down the garden, he never lifted his head but just went on playing as if she had never spoken.

What happened was that Mum came to the door and called to Bobby, 'Bobby, come into the house. I want you to wash your hands and face because we're going out.' Then she went back indoors and waited for Bobby to appear but he never did.

Back went Mum to the door and shouted again, 'Bobby, come in at once and get cleaned up.' Still Bobby didn't come. So Mum went a third time to the door. This time she shouted very loudly, 'Bobby, come into the house this minute.'

When he heard his Mum shouting like that, Bobby knew that he daren't put off any longer and into the house he went. Mum was angry and she said, 'Bobby, why did you take so long to come in?'

Bobby replied, 'It was because I didn't hear you the first two times you called.'

Of course, saying that proved to Mum that Bobby had heard her all along, otherwise he wouldn't have known that she had called him three times. So Bobby didn't get away with it. His attempted excuse didn't work.

Sometimes we may attempt excuses for not obeying God when he calls us but it's no good trying to pretend where God is concerned. He always knows the truth about us.

Bobby embarrasses Mum and Dad

It was when his Mum and Dad were having visitors one night for an evening meal that Bobby let them down rather badly. It was not that he did something terrible. In fact he didn't really do anything wrong but he made them feel very embarrassed.

The visitors weren't people who came very often for a meal. In fact Mum and Dad didn't really like them all that well but Mrs. Robinson is Mum's cousin and she feels she ought to invite them along occasionally for that reason.

When it came time for the meal, they all sat down at the table. Bobby was there, too, because it was Friday evening and since there was no school the next day, he didn't need to go to bed as early as usual. When they were all in their places, Dad said, 'I'll say grace before we start.'

Before he could begin, Mrs. Robinson said, 'It's nice to have Bobby at the table with us. Perhaps he could say the grace.'

That was a poser and no mistake because Dad always said the grace and Bobby had never done it before. But Mum didn't want her cousin to think that Bobby wasn't clever enough to say grace and so she said, 'Yes, that would be nice. Bobby hasn't ever said grace before but he'll say it tonight since you are here, won't you, Bobby?'

Bobby was all flustered. He didn't want to refuse his mum but he just didn't know what he was supposed to say.

'But what will I say, Mum?' he asked.

'Just say what you heard Dad say this morning,' she replied.

They all shut their eyes and Bobby took a deep breath. Then he began.

'Goodness gracious,' he said, just as he had heard Dad say at breakfast time, 'why did you go and invite those boring Robinsons to come tonight?'

Well, that caused a bit of an upset. Mum and Dad were terribly embarrassed indeed. Bobby had let them down badly in front of their visitors, even though it was largely their own fault.

One thing we can depend on is that God will never let us down, even when we are badly at fault.

Bobby goes on strike

One day Bobby was watching television when the news came on. The broadcaster began telling about some people who were going on strike because they felt they weren't getting paid enough money for the work they were doing. It made Bobby think.

He said to himself, 'Perhaps I should be getting paid more for the jobs I do for Mum. I think I'll ask her for a rise and if I don't get it, I'll go on strike.'

Off he went to Mum. 'Mum,' he said, 'I think I deserve an increase in my pocket money. After all, I do quite a lot to help you don't I, and sweets and things keep getting dearer. How about it?'

'I'm afraid not,' said Mum. 'Your pocket money was increased not very long ago. You're not going to get another increase just yet.'

'Well, then,' said Bobby, 'if you're not going to give me more pocket money, I'll just have to go on strike. I won't be doing any more jobs for you until you change your mind.'

Bobby expected Mum to argue with him. He was rather afraid she might be angry. Instead Mum was as nice as nice could be when she spoke. 'Bobby,' she said, 'I think a strike might be a good idea. I've never gone on strike myself before now but I think I'll try it. In fact, I'll just start my strike right away.'

No sooner had she said this than she stopped peeling the potatoes, dried her hands, took a book from the bookcase, plopped into an armchair and began to read her book.

'I'm so happy about this,' Mum said. 'I've always wanted to read this book but I never seemed able to find the time. Now that I'm on strike, I'll have plenty of time to read it through.'

Bobby's mouth had dropped open. He was quite taken aback. He had never expected anything like this. 'But what about our dinner?' he said. 'How is that going to get made?'

'I'm afraid there won't be any dinner,' was Mum's reply. 'I'll not be making it anyway for I'm on strike, remember, just like you.'

'That's not fair,' Bobby complained. 'YOU can't go on strike. We can't manage if you go on strike.'

Mum was only pretending, of course. She didn't really mean to go on strike and Bobby got his dinner all right. But it made him think. It made him appreciate all the more what his Mum does for him.

Fortunately for us all, God never goes on strike. He just keeps loving us and offering to help us all the time.

Bobby asks me riddles

Bobby is very fond of riddles as well as jokes and he tries out most of them on me. He likes nothing better than to ask me a riddle that I can't answer. When I do know the answer, he always looks surprised. Perhaps he thinks grown-ups are not supposed to know much about riddles. Here are some of his.

'When can you drop a full tumbler and not spill any water?'

'When the tumbler is full of milk.'

'When can three large men get under one small umbrella and not get wet?'

'When it's not raining.'

I think one of the daftest riddles he ever asked me was when he said, 'What's the difference between an elephant and a biscuit?'

I had to say, 'Bobby, I don't know. What is the difference between an elephant and a biscuit?'

'Well,' he replied, with a big laugh, 'you can't dip an elephant in your tea.'

He loves to catch me out and one day he managed it rather well. 'You know me rather well, don't you?' he said.

'Yes, Bobby,' I replied, 'I know you well.'

'Will you always remember me?' he asked next.

'Yes, I'll always remember you,' I said. 'How could I ever forget you?'

All of a sudden Bobby said, 'Knock, knock.' I thought I could see one of his jokes coming, so I said, 'Who's there?'

'There you are,' Bobby shouted gleefully, 'you've forgotten me already.'

Bobby was just playing a joke on me. But it would be a terrible thing if someone you were friendly with forgot you. One person who will never forget us is God. He always remembers us and always will. Jesus tells us that and we can depend on it.

Bobby doesn't laugh at the Minister's joke

Bobby and his minister get on very well together and they often tell jokes to each other. Bobby enjoys this.

The minister knows that Bobby is fond of 'Doctor' jokes and one day he said to Bobby, 'Bobby, I've got a new ''Doctor'' joke for you. Here it is.'

Patient: 'Doctor, doctor, I'm feeling so depressed because no one ever takes any notice of me.'

Doctor: 'Next patient, please.' The minister expected Bobby to laugh out loud but he didn't laugh at all. As a matter of fact he looked as if he was going to burst into tears.

'What's wrong, Bobby?' said the minister. 'Did you not like that joke? I thought myself it was quite a good one.'

'No, I didn't like it at all,' replied Bobby. 'It's not a funny joke at all. It's really very sad. It's awful when no one pays any attention to you. I know because no one takes any notice of me.'

'Come on now, Bobby,' said the minister. 'That's not true. What makes you think it is.'

'Well,' said Bobby, 'I wasn't picked for the school football team today. I wasn't chosen to give out the pencils to my school class today. And I wasn't given the chance to take up the offering at the Sunday School last Sunday—and it should have been my turn. Nobody cares for me. Everybody ignores me.'

'Now, now, Bobby,' the minister said, 'cheer up. Of course people care for you. I care for you. Your parents care for you. Your little sister cares for you. You mustn't get down in the dumps because you didn't get into the football team this week. You'll probably be in it again next week. And you'll get your turn at the other things, too. I'm sure of that. Just as I'm sure that God will never ignore you or forget you. Even when you're feeling down, you may be sure that God still loves you.'

'I feel a lot better now,' said Bobby. 'Tell me that doctor joke again, please. I think I'll laugh at it this time.'

Bobby gives me an 'objects' riddle

Bobby one day had a different kind of riddle for me. How pleased he was when I couldn't answer it.

When I called in to see him, I could tell at once that he was very excited about something. I soon discovered why. He had his riddle all prepared and was desperately keen to try it out on me.

'Do you know what this is?' he asked as he showed me a tin of coke.

'It's a tin of coke,' I said.

'And what are these?' he said, as he fished out an umbrella and a Bible. 'An umbrella and a Bible,' I replied, wondering what was coming.

'You're giving me very easy riddles today,' I said.

Bobby laughed out loud. 'I haven't come to the riddle yet,' he said. 'Here it is now. What do these three things have in common?'

'What DO they have in common?' I wondered. 'A tin of coke, an umbrella and a Bible. They are all so different.'

I thought and I thought but I couldn't come up with the answer. And all the time Bobby was smiling triumphantly and hopping from foot to foot in great glee.

At last I decided I would have to give up.

'I give in, Bobby,' I said. 'You'll have to tell me the answer. What do they have in common?'

'Well,' Bobby shouted, 'this is what they have in common. None of them is any good until it is opened.'

What a good answer and how true. We can't get a drink of coke out of the can until it is opened. The umbrella won't keep off the rain unless it is opened. And it's only when we open our Bible that we can read in it the story of Jesus.

Bobby stirs the Christmas cake

Bobby's Mum bakes their Christmas cake herself. She is very good at it and it always has a gorgeous taste. Bobby is very fond of his Mum's Christmas cake, especially the cherries in it. He loves cherries.

He also likes to watch Mum making the cake. One year he was able to help. He was standing watching as Mum mixed things together in a baking bowl and then began to stir them. He noticed that she had a big bowl of cherries on the table, too. They were to be added to the mixture later.

'Bobby,' said Mum, 'how would you like to give me a hand? I want to go and make a telephone call. Will you keep stirring the cake while I do it? I won't be long.' Then she added—I think it may have been to keep Bobby interested, 'There's a saying—I don't know whether or not it's true—that if you make a wish when you are stirring a Christmas cake, that wish will be granted.' Off Mum went to the telephone and Bobby started to stir.

When Mum returned a few minutes later Bobby shouted out, 'That saying IS true, Mum. I made a wish when I started the cake and it has come true already. I wished that I could eat all those cherries that were in the bowl and it has happened.'

Sure enough, when Mum looked, the bowl was empty. She was not very pleased, however, because she saw through Bobby's trick. He was just making the saying about the wish an excuse. He wanted to eat the cherries and he thought he would get away with doing so by blaming it all on the wish. But Mum knew that it was really Bobby himself who was to blame.

Bobby was being selfish and at the same time trying to cover up his selfishness. That is something many of us try to do at times. We may sometimes succeed in covering it up as far as other people are concerned but we can never hide the truth from God.

Bobby and the Crabs' Sunday School

Sometimes the stories Bobby's minister tells the children strike right home to Bobby. That was the case when he told them about the Crabs' Sunday School.

Mum had been having a bit of a struggle with Bobby for the past two weeks. He had developed an annoying habit of nodding his head instead of saying 'Yes'. Mum spent a lot of time trying to get him out of this habit.

'Stop nodding your head like that in answer to a question. It's much more polite to say ''yes'', and that's what I'd like you to do,' she would say. Bobby always agreed with her. For a short time he would do as she wanted. Then he would go back to nodding his head again. Mum didn't know what to do next until the story of the Crabs' Sunday School came along and made all the difference. This is the story:

One day the fishes in the sea became worried about the way the crabs walked. The fishes themselves swam in a straight line but the crabs walked sideways. The fishes did what grown-up people often do when they are puzzled. They formed a committee to look into the problem.

Eventually the committee decided to start a Sunday School for baby crabs to teach them to walk straight—for baby crabs only, because they knew that the habits of adult crabs would be more difficult to change. A notice was sent all round the sea bed announcing—in fishy language, of course—that a Sunday School for baby crabs would start the next Sunday afternoon at 3 o'clock.

The next Sunday afternoon crabs came from every direction to the Sunday School, all walking sideways. The committee had selected certain clever fish to teach the baby crabs to walk straight. For an hour they marched them up and down until they were all walking as straight as straight could be. Then they were sent home and told to come again the following Sunday. Off they went walking straight and their teachers were very pleased.

Next Sunday afternoon the little crabs flocked back to the Sunday School but they were all walking sideways again. The teachers were very disappointed but set to work teaching the crabs all over gain. Once more at the end of the lesson the crabs went off home walking straight.

A week later they came back again—walking sideways. Again their teachers marched them up and down and sent them away walking straight. And again they came back walking sideways.

This happened for a few more weeks. Then the fishes decided to hold another committee meeting. After it they sent another notice round the sea bed. The notice said: 'The Crabs' Sunday School is being stopped because it's no good walking straight on Sundays if you are content to walk sideways through the week.'

It's a bit like following Jesus on Sundays but behaving any old way the rest of the week.

Bobby, I can tell you, always says 'yes' now instead of nodding his head, even when Mum isn't there.

Bobby gives up halfway round

When Bobby went to Millport for his holidays he was desperately keen to cycle round the island. Millport is situated on the Isle of Cumbrae in the Firth of Clyde. The main road on the island follows the coast line and goes all the way round. It's a distance of nearly eleven miles.

It was a favourite pastime of holiday makers to hire a bicycle and 'go round the island'. Bobby was determined to do it, too. This was a big thing for a little boy to do but he had a bike on hire for the whole month and he practised hard. Every day he cycled a bit further than the day before. Then one day he announced to Mum, 'I'm going to try to cycle right round the island today.'

'Are you sure you can manage it?' asked Mum. 'It's a long way for a small boy like you.'

'Yes, Mum,' said Bobby, 'I'm sure I can do it. I've been practising really hard. Cheerio. I'm off.' And away he went.

Mum said to herself, 'I do hope he manages to do it. He'll be so disappointed if he doesn't.' She knew it would take him quite a long time to cycle all the way and when more and more time passed, she began to think he must be succeeding in going all the way round after all.

Just then Bobby arrived back. Mum could tell at a glance that he had failed to do it. His face was so glum.

'Did you not manage it?' she asked.

'No, Mum, I didn't. I thought at first I was going to be all right but by the time I got halfway round I realised it was going to be too far. So I had to turn round and come back home.'

Poor Bobby. He was HALFWAY round before he turned to come back. He wouldn't have had any further to cycle if he had kept going forward than he had by going back. If only he had kept going.

Sometimes we may be tempted to abandon something worthwhile when it would be just as easy to keep on going. Jesus certainly would like us to keep on keeping on in his service.

Bobby gets a surprise

Bobby loves surprises. He loves all the excitement of opening his Christmas presents and his birthday presents. He loves all that kind of thing. He loves all sorts of other pleasant surprises, too.

Like the one he got when Mum handed him a little parcel one lunchtime.

'A lady along the street handed this in for you,' said Mum. 'She said it was a little thank you for always giving her a smile on your way to school.'

Bobby tore open the parcel at once and found that it contained a box of smarties. It was a lovely surprise because smarties are one of his favourite sweets.

'I'll take them to school with me,' he thought, and put them in his pocket. But as he was going out the door, he changed his mind and decided to leave them at home so that he would have them to come back to. He turned round and put the packet on the kitchen table. Mum was upstairs with Susan so he shouted up to her, 'I'm not taking the smarties after all. I've left them on the table for later.' And off he went.

Poor Bobby was going to have another surprise when he came back home and this time it wasn't a pleasant one. Mum hadn't been able to hear him clearly when he shouted up the stairs. She thought he said, 'I'm not taking the smarties after all. I've left them on the table for my sister.'

The result was that when Bobby came home from school looking forward to eating his smarties, it was to find the packet empty. Susan had eaten them all. That was a surprise all right but not one he enjoyed.

Life is full of surprises. It is good to get a pleasant surprise but not so good to get an unpleasant one.

The biggest surprise the world has ever known was the first Easter and it was a very happy one. On Good Friday the friends of Jesus were broken-hearted because he had been killed. But on the Sunday morning they got a wonderful surprise when they discovered that God had made Jesus alive again. He is alive still.

Bobby sets an example

One afternoon when I called at Bobby's house, Bobby was standing in the front garden craning his head back to look up at the sky. I wondered what he could be looking at so I tilted my head back, too, and looked up. I stared and stared but could see nothing special.

At last I said to Bobby, 'What are you looking at? Is there something specially interesting up there that I'm failing to see?'

'No,' Bobby replied, with a laugh, 'there's nothing special to see. I was playing a trick on you. I heard on the radio about a man who suddenly stopped in the middle of a busy street and began to stare up into the sky. In a minute lots of other people were stopped and looking up into the sky. But there was nothing to see. The man was just playing a trick and it worked. I just wondered if it would work with you. It did, didn't it?'

'It certainly did,' I said, for I was quite impressed. 'I wonder if it would work in your street. How about trying it?'

Bobby didn't need a second invitation. Before I could regret speaking so rashly, I was standing in the street beside Bobby and both of us were gazing intently up into the sky. In no time at all we were the centre of a group of people all staring up just like we were.

By now I was beginning to feel embarrassed at the thought of having to explain to the others what it was all about. Quietly I took Bobby's arm and the two of us slipped quietly through the garden gate and into Bobby's house before anyone could start to ask awkward questions.

That was a harmless bit of fun but it shows how easily people may be led to follow someone else's example. We ought, therefore, to be as careful as possible to show the best example we can at all times. The best way to make sure of this is to take Jesus as OUR example and to ask his help in following him day by day.

Mum tells Bobby a story

When Bobby came home from school, Mum knew at once that something was troubling him. He looked so down in the mouth. 'What's wrong, Bobby?' she asked.

'Some boys were making fun of me at school because I go to church and Sunday School,' he replied. 'They said they wouldn't waste their time doing that and they laughed at me for doing it.'

'But you know, Bobby, don't you, that going to church and Sunday School is the right thing to do and you enjoy it anyway.'

'Yes,' Bobby said, 'but I don't like the boys laughing at me for it.'

'Sometimes,' said Mum, 'we've just got to do what we know to be right even though it isn't pleasing everybody. Let me tell you a story.'

Bobby knows that Mum's stories are always good, so he settled down to listen and this is the story he was told.

A farmer was taking his donkey to market to be sold. Along with his son he set off walking alongside the donkey. They met some people going in the opposite direction. As they passed, the farmer heard them say, 'Look at those silly people walking when they could be riding on the donkey.'

At this the farmer and his son got on the donkey's back and continued on their way. Soon they met some other people who shouted at them, 'You cruel pair. Imagine two of you on one poor donkey. Think shame.'

At this the farmer dismounted and on they went with only his son on the donkey. The next group of people they met were heard to say, 'Imagine that selfish boy riding while his poor father has to walk.'

The farmer said to his son, 'I'm afraid we haven't got it right yet. You get off and I'll get on.' So they changed over and on they went. But they were still not pleasing everybody. The next people they met criticised them, too. 'Look at that selfish man riding on the donkey while his poor son has to walk.'

The farmer got off the donkey's back and said, 'We've tried everything else to please people. There's only one way left. You and I will need to carry the donkey. Surely no one can criticise us then.' So they tied the donkey's legs together, slung him over a pole and carried him between them the rest of the way.

When they reached the market, all the people there laughed and jeered when they saw them carrying the donkey. 'How silly can you get?' they shouted. 'Donkeys are meant to carry people, not the other way round.'

The farmer shook his head sadly as he said to his son, 'Clearly it's impossible to please everybody. From now on I'm just going to do what I see to be right, whatever other people think.'

Bobby thought it was a very good story and its lesson helped him.

Bobby takes a tumble

Summer is the time of year that Bobby likes best. He likes it most of all when he's on holiday and especially if the sun is shining. But he likes it sometimes in the winter, too. He likes it then if it snows or if it becomes really frosty.

He simply loves it when it is frosty enough for him and his chums at school to make a 'slide' in the playground. When it is frosty enough, they rub and rub with their feet on the frosty surface of the playground until it becomes really slippery. Then they are able to slide up and down on it as if they were on a skating rink.

Bobby loves it then. He loves to slide over the ice and he likes to slide as fast as he can. He is very good at it, too. His balance is spendid and that really led to his downfall one frosty day. He had been having a great time at the morning interval, sliding in the playground with his friends. He was full of it when he went home for his lunch and was in a great hurry to get back to the school so that he could have a real go before afternoon classes began.

He gobbled down his lunch as fast as he could and got ready to leave. 'I'm going back to school now, Mum,' he said.

'But you're far too early,' Mum said.

'I know but I want to use the slide. It's great fun.'

'Well, see and be careful,' Mum warned. 'It can be dangerous sliding on the ice. Take care you don't fall.'

'Don't worry,' Bobby scoffed. 'I'm very good at sliding on the ice. I won't fall.' But he did. As soon as he reached the playground he went on the slide. Every time he went down it he became more and more confident. He became so confident that he began to try fancy tricks like sliding on one foot and waving the other one in the air.

This was all right for a time or two until he became too confident. He was sliding down the slide as fast as he could with one foot waving vigorously behind him when all of a sudden he lost his balance and fell down with a crash. Luckily no bones were broken but it was very painful. What made Bobby feel worse was that the other boys laughed out loud.

When I heard that tale I was reminded of something St. Paul says in his first letter to the Corinthians. He is warning Christians about becoming too cocky and thinking they can live their lives well enough without the help of Jesus.

This is what he actually says: 'If you feel sure you are standing firm, beware. You may fall.'

Bobby looks on the bright side

Bobby and Susan had a disagreement one day. It was all over a bottle of lemonade.

Mum said to Susan, 'There's an unfinished bottle of lemonade in the pantry. Is there much in it?' 'Not much,' said Susan. 'It's half empty.'

Just then Bobby came in. Mum said to him, 'We'll need to get some more lemonade today. Susan tells me there's not much left in the bottle.'

'Oh,' said Bobby, 'there's quite a lot left. The bottle is half full.'

Susan said the bottle was half empty. Bobby said it was half full. They were both right for half empty is just the same amount as half full. But they were different ways of looking at the same thing. Bobby's way was the cheerier way. He had chosen to look on the bright side.

You could say the same about the postcard he sent to his grandmother from their holidays. His mum had sent a postcard to Gran at the same time. In fact her postcard and Bobby's arrived by the same post.

Mum's postcard said, 'We're enjoying our holiday very much but there has been rain every day.' Bobby's postcard said, 'We're having a great time and there's been sunshine every day.'

In fact there had been both rain and sunshine every single day of the holiday. Both Mum and Bobby were perfectly correct in what they said on their postcards. But wasn't Bobby's way of looking at the weather a better way than his Mum's? He was choosing to look on the bright side.

It makes life a lot happier both for other people and for ourselves when we choose to look on the bright side of things. And there always is a bright side no matter what may be happening to us so long as we remember that God loves us and has given us Jesus to be our Friend.

Bobby says 'Goodbye, God'

Bobby was all excited. The very next day he was to go on his summer holidays to the seaside. Mum, Dad and Susan were, of course, going as well. Bobby had been looking forward to it for ages and now the time had nearly arrived.

All day long he'd been hopping about supposedly helping Mum with the packing but really just getting in her way most of the time. For instance, he kept coming to her with another of his toys that he thought he would like to take.

'Bobby,' Mum told him more than once, 'we can't possibly take all your toys. We simply haven't room. You've got to make up your mind which ones are most important to you. If you want me to put in this one you've just brought along, something else will have to be taken out. It's up to you.'

That was how it had gone all day. But now it was bedtime. Most of the packing was done and Mum was standing beside Bobby's bed as he said his prayers. She listened with interest as he said all the usual things like asking God to bless Mum, Dad and Susan.

She got a surprise, however, when he came to the end of his prayer and he heard him say, 'And now, God, I'll have to say goodbye to you for a while. I'm going on my holidays tomorrow and since I'll be away from you for the next month, I'll not be able to speak to you till I get back. But I'll be in touch then.'

Mum felt she had to try to put Bobby right. 'Bobby,' she said, 'we don't leave God behind when we go away from home. God is everywhere and he'll still be with us when we are on our holidays. We are never out of his sight or away from his care.'

Bobby and the Christmas tree

Bobby was most upset when Dad put out the Christmas tree to be collected with the rubbish. He was so upset that he cried.

That morning Dad had said, 'Tonight is Twelfth Night so we must get all the Christmas decorations down after I get home from work.' That night as soon as he'd had his dinner, Dad began. In no time at all the Christmas tree was stripped of its decorations. Mum carefully packed them up to be stored away along with the tree lights for next year's use. Then Dad picked up the Christmas tree and carried it outside. He put it down beside the dustbin so that the refuse collectors would take it away when they came to collect the rubbish.

That's when Bobby started to cry.

'What's making you cry?' Dad asked.

'I'm sad,' said Bobby, 'because there's no Christmas any more. You've just put the last of it on the rubbish heap. I wish we could have Christmas all the time.'

'You needn't cry about it,' Dad said, 'because in a very real sense Christmas is never away from us. Christmas is, as you know, the birthday of Jesus and Jesus is with us all the time.' That seemed to satisfy Bobby.

Later that same day Dad came upon Bobby making his little sister cry. Susan had been playing happily with some of her toys when Bobby took the toys from her. 'I want to play with these,' he said.

'But they are MY toys,' cried Susan. 'I want to play with them.'

'Well, you can't get them,' said Bobby, 'and that's that.' That's when Susan began to cry and that's just when Dad came on the scene.

'Look here, Bobby,' he said, 'you're the very one who wanted to have Christmas all the year round. And here the Christmas season is newly over and already you've stopped showing any Christmas spirit to your sister.'

The message of Christmas is for every day of the year. So is the Christmas spirit of love and friendship.

Bobby renders Mum an account

One day Bobby's chum, Jimmy, said to him, 'Let's go to the sweet shop and buy something. I've got 20p to spend. My mum gave it to me for helping her with the dishes yesterday.'

Bobby was very pleased to go with Jimmy to the sweet shop and afterwards to help him eat the sweets. But he could not help thinking to himself, 'I help my mum often with the dishes and I help her with other things too. She ought to be paying me for the things I do over and above my pocket money. I think I'll go home and make up an account to let her know how much she owes me.'

That's just what he did. He went home and wrote it all down, slowly and carefully, on a sheet of paper. Then he handed the paper to Mum. She got a surprise when she read what he had written:

Bobby's account to Mum for yesterday.

For running an errand to the lady next door 10p
For helping with the dishes twice...20p
For tidying up my room when told to 20p
For keeping Susan quiet when Mum was telephoning...............10p
                                                        Total   60p

When she had read it, Mum said to Bobby, 'I'd better give you my account, too.' A little later she handed him a sheet of paper. This is what IT said:

For bringing Bobby into the world................................no charge
For looking after Bobby all his life ....no charge
For bandaging Bobby's skinned knees many times ....no charge
For loving Bobby even when he was in a bad mood.........no charge
                                                        Total   nothing

Bobby felt so ashamed. He realised that he owed Mum far, far more than she owed him and yet she did not ask for any payment.

That's what most mothers are like. That's why, for instance, we have Mother's Day. It's so that we can give thanks for our mothers and their love for us. And so that we can give thanks to God for his love, too.

Bobby likes jokes

Bobby is very fond of jokes and likes nothing better than to try them out on me. One day he happened along with a collection of 'doctor' jokes and he wasted no time before he started firing them off at me in rapid succession. Here are some of them.

'Doctor, I keep thinking I'm a pair of curtains.'

'You must pull yourself together.'

'Doctor, I've swallowed my mouth organ.'

'Aren't you lucky you weren't playing the piano?'

'Doctor, I sometimes imagine I'm a dustman.'

'Don't talk rubbish.'

'Doctor, I keep thinking I'm a snooker ball.'

'Go to the end of the queue.'

Bobby fairly enjoyed telling me these jokes, especially when he realised I hadn't heard them before. Then suddenly he said to me, 'Did Jesus like jokes? Do you think he would have laughed at mine?'

'Yes, Bobby,' I replied, 'I'm sure Jesus did like jokes and I'm sure he would have laughed at yours.'

There is no doubt that Jesus had a good sense of humour. Some people, called Pharisees, used to criticise him because they said he and his friends laughed too much. These Pharisees thought that being religious meant being dull and solemn. Even today some people think that being a Christian means being miserable. But Jesus tells us that those who truly follow him will be really happy. He says he'll help them to enjoy life.

Bobby has an argument

Bobby's best friend, Jimmy, is a regular attender at his church and
Sunday School just as Bobby is. They both enjoy it and both of them like
their ministers very much.

One day they had an argument about which minister was better than
the other. It was a friendly argument but vigorous, too.

'My minister's a better minister than yours is,' said Jimmy.

'No, he's not,' replied Bobby. 'My minister is better than yours.'

That was how the argument started but it didn't finish there. Oh, no.

'My minister tells good stories to the children,' said Jimmy next.

'So does my minister,' was Bobby's response, 'and he tells funny
ones, too.'

'My minister can tell funny stories, too,' came back Jimmy, 'and
what's more, he's a good singer.'

'My minister's both a good singer and a good whistler,' said Bobby.

'That's nothing,' said Jimmy, 'my minister's a good whistler as
well—and he can play the piano.'

Bobby was nearly stumped this time because his minister doesn't play
the piano. He was speechless for nearly a whole minute, then a smile of
triumph appeared on his face and he shouted, 'Maybe so, but my
minister's better looking than yours. My minister is tall and slim but your
minister is short and fat'.

It was Jimmy's turn to be speechless for a minute—but just for a
minute. He wasn't wanting to admit defeat either. This is what he came
away with next. 'That's all very well but my minister would be every bit
as tall and slim as yours if he was pulled out.'

That was the end of the argument—a drawn contest, I think.

Jimmy's defence of his minister is worth thinking about. In another
sense from the way Jimmy had in mind, lots of people are just waiting to
be 'pulled out', needing some help to develop into the best they could be.

Jesus is able to help us make the best of ourselves if we put ourselves
into his hands.

Bobby's bad memory

Bobby has a good memory for lots of things, especially the things that interest him. His memory is sometimes not so good for other things, especially if they don't interest him very much.

One day, for instance, Mum asked him to run an errand to the little shop at the corner of the street. 'Run along, Bobby, please, and get me a packet of salt and you can get yourself a packet of smarties,' she said, as she gave him some money. 'All right, Mum,' Bobby said, 'and thank you for the smarties.'

In a very short time he was back and handed Mum a packet of SUGAR. 'You silly boy,' said Mum, 'It was salt you had to get, not sugar.'

'I'm sorry, Mum,' said Bobby, 'I knew I had to get a packet of something but I couldn't remember what it was so I thought it must be sugar.'

'Tell me, Bobby,' said Mum. 'did you remember to buy your smarties?'

'Oh, yes,' said Bobby, 'I got them all right and they're very good.'

'Isn't it strange,' Mum said, 'that you could remember one of the things I asked you to get but couldn't remember the other? I wonder why you forgot my salt when you didn't forget your smarties?'

Bobby thought hard for a minute, then he said. 'I don't really know, unless it's because I'm so fond of smarties.'

It's certainly true that we're not likely to forget something or someone we're very fond of.

This also is certain, that God is so fond of us that he'll never forget any one of us even if we forget him.

Bobby and the reminder

Grown-ups can be absent-minded. We all know that. But children can be absent-minded, too. Bobby sometimes is, anyway.

One day Mum said to him, 'Bobby, on your way home from school will you call in at the shop on the corner and get me a loaf of bread?'

'All right,' said Bobby, 'I'll do that.' But when he arrived home from school he wasn't carrying any bread.

'Where's the bread I asked you to get for me?' said Mum.

Bobby's hand flew up to his mouth and he said in dismay, 'I'm sorry. I forgot all about it.'

The same thing happened on another day soon afterwards. Bobby agreed to collect a loaf of bread on the way home from school but forgot about it.

A few days later Mum said to Bobby as he was getting ready to go to school, 'Bobby, I would like you to get me a loaf of bread on your way home but since you've forgotten twice already to do this, I'm going to give you something to help you remember.' And she tied a piece of string round one of his fingers.

'That string,' she said, 'will remind you to get bread on your way home.'

'What a good idea,' Bobby said, 'I surely can't forget this time.'

But once again Bobby came home from school without the bread.

'Where's that loaf you were supposed to bring with you?' asked Mum.

'I'm afraid I didn't remember to get it,' said Bobby.

'Did the string round your finger not remind you?' Mum asked.

'Well,' said Bobby, 'I looked at the string several times and I knew it was to remind me of something. But I couldn't remember what that something was.'

Reminders are helpful things but they have to make it clear what they are meant to remind us of.

That's why the Christian symbol of an empty cross is so helpful. It reminds us so clearly of how Jesus gave his life for our sakes and then was made alive again by God.

Bobby forgets to say thanks

Bobby had been looking forward to the Sunday School Christmas party for weeks. He was looking forward to the games they would be playing. He was looking forward to the food they would get to eat. Most of all he was looking forward to seeing Santa Claus and to getting a present from him.

When the day of the party came he was very excited. He could hardly wait for it to come to two o'clock in the afternoon when the party was to start.

Mum was a little bit excited, too. But she was also a little bit worried. She wanted Bobby to be on his best behaviour. In particular she wanted him to be sure to say 'Thank you' to Santa Claus when he received his present.

The trouble was that recently Bobby had often been forgetting to say 'Thank you' when he should have been saying it. Mum was worried in case he created a bad impression at the party by forgetting to say thanks to Santa. That was why she said to Bobby just before she left him outside the church hall, 'Don't forget to say ''Thank you, Santa'' when he gives you your present. Now, what are you going to say to him?'

Bobby replied, 'I'm going to say ''Thank you, Santa''.'

'Well, don't forget,' Mum said again—and off she went.

All the way up the path to the hall door, Bobby kept repeating to himself, 'Thank you, Santa. Thank you, Santa.' Just as he entered the hall, a new boy spoke to him and said, 'What's your name?'

'Thank you, Santa' was Bobby's answer. When his teacher asked him, 'What kind of cake would you like?' Bobby's answer again was, 'Thank you, Santa.' When another teacher asked him, 'What game would you like to play next?' Bobby still replied, 'Thank you, Santa.' Nearly every time anyone spoke to him that was what he said in answer. He was so determined to say what his mum wanted him to say.

The strange thing was that when Santa did come and handed over his present to him, Bobby was so excited that he just grabbed the present from Santa's hand and rushed back to his seat without uttering one word.

This was a great pity because it's always good to say thanks to someone who has given us a present or done a kindness to us. It's especially good to say thanks to God, for he has given us a lot. He has even given his son, Jesus, to be our Friend and Saviour.

Bobby and the best part of the story

Bobby and his Grandpa get on very well together. Perhaps it's partly because Grandpa is always willing to play games with Bobby. He's always ready, too, to listen to whatever Bobby has to say—and that's usually a lot.

Bobby talks to his Grandpa almost non-stop as he tries to tell him all he's been doing since they last saw each other. He tells him where he's been, about the people he's seen, the children he's been playing with and just about everything else he can think of.

Grandpa listens to it all. Occasionally he puts in a word or two here and there. Sometimes he asks a question. But mostly he just nods his head.

If Bobby sees his Grandpa on a Sunday evening or on a Monday he's sure to tell him what the Sunday School lesson was about. One Sunday evening—it was Easter Day—he could hardly wait to say 'hello' before he started.

'Grandpa', he said, 'today's story was terribly exciting—and sad, too. It was about how wicked men plotted against Jesus. They told lies about him and got him arrested. Do you know, Grandpa, they got him condemned to die and he was crucified to death by Roman soldiers. It was so sad it made me want to cry.'

Bobby went very quiet for a minute or two after that. Grandpa was surprised at this because Bobby is hardly ever quiet. But he realised that Bobby was thinking about the story he had just been telling him for his face was very solemn. So he said nothing.

Suddenly Bobby's face changed. He smiled and started to speak again. 'Grandpa,' he said, and he sounded more excited than ever. 'Grandpa, I nearly forgot to tell you the best part of the story. Jesus didn't stay dead. God made him alive again. He is alive now and he wants to be our Saviour and Friend.'

Bobby and Susan on the Ghost Train

When Mum and Dad took them to the carnival, Bobby and Susan had a marvellous time. They enjoyed all the colour and excitement. What is more, Dad gave them quite a lot of money to spend. That meant they were able to do a lot of enjoyable things.

First of all they bought some candy floss. As they walked around eating it, they made up their minds how they would spend the rest of their money. Some things, they knew, were not for them because they were too small. They would have to wait until they were older before they could try them. But there was plenty that was suitable for children of their age and they had a great time.

They still had some money left when they came to the Ghost Train. As they stood looking at it, Mum said, 'I think that might be too scary for you. That little train takes you into dark places where skeletons and other creepy things jump out at you.'

'I think we would enjoy that, wouldn't we, Susan?' said brave Bobby.

Susan agreed. So they paid their money and boarded the Ghost Train. Dad and Mum went with them in case it might frighten them too much.

Just as Mum had warned it would be, Bobby found it really scary. They were in pitch darkness most of the time and every now and again a ghostly figure would suddenly jump up in front of them out of the darkness. Lots of times Bobby let out a squeal of fright but Susan never uttered a sound.

When they came to the end of the run and got off the train, Bobby said to Susan, 'I never heard you scream once. Did the ghosts and the skeletons not frighten you?'

'No,' said Susan, 'they didn't frighten me at all because I didn't see them. I kept my eyes shut all the time. Did they frighten you?'

'Yes,' Bobby admitted, 'they frightened me a lot but I was holding Dad's hand so it was all right.'

Some people try to shut their eyes to the frightening things of life. But that doesn't make them go away. If, however, we hold tight to God's loving hand, it will be all right whatever frightening things are there.

Bobby forgets Susan

Bobby had been invited to the birthday party of the boy next door. Susan had also been invited and they were both delighted to be going. Children's birthday parties don't always take place in the house nowadays but this one was to be in the house. Since it was just next door, Mum said to Bobby, 'Since the party is next door, I'll not need to take you there. You can take Susan round with you.'

So when Bobby and Susan had been got ready for the party and Mum was satisfied they were looking their best, off they went. Bobby held Susan's hand in his until they reached their neighbour's door. As soon as he rang the bell, the door was opened. In they went to join the others and once everyone was there the party got started.

It was a lovely party. The food was good and the games were splendid. The time passed so swiftly that it was a surprise to Bobby when the lady of the house announced that the party was over. He was disappointed that it had come to an end.

Just then he realised what the time was. His favourite television programme was just about to start. He knew that if he hurried home he would be just in time for it. So he just took time to say, 'Thanks for a lovely party,' before he scuttled back to his own house.

As soon as he was in the door he rushed over to the television set but before he had time to switch it on, Mum said in a very loud voice, 'Bobby, where is Susan? Surely you haven't come away without her?'

But that was just what Bobby had done. He had forgotten all about his own sister. It was a terrible thing to do. Yet we can all be guilty at times of forgetting important things and important people.

Sometimes we may even forget God.

But he never forgets us.

Bobby develops sore feet

Once Bobby learned how to do it himself, he refused any longer to let his Mum help him put on his clothes. He insisted on doing it every day without any assistance whatsoever.

To begin with he often found this very difficult but he would never admit it. Sometimes that caused problems. There was, for instance, that awful morning when he couldn't stand up and thought his legs were paralysed. What had happened was that, sitting on the bed as he dressed, he had put both feet through the same trouser leg. As soon as he tried to stand up he fell over and couldn't get up (My Friend Bobby p. 48).

Bobby had a fright on another day, too, that was also because of a mistake he made when dressing. But it was not the same mistake.

He came limping down the stairs from his bedroom and he was crying. 'What's wrong?' Mum asked.

'My feet are hurting me,' said Bobby. 'They're hurting me so much I can hardly walk.'

'What's made your feet sore?' Mum asked. 'Did you knock them against something? Perhaps you got them hurt playing football.'

'No, Mum,' answered Bobby. 'I haven't done anything at all to hurt them. But they're very sore and I don't know what's wrong with them.'

'Sit down,' Mum said with a worried frown. 'Let me have a look at your feet'.

As soon as Bobby sat down, Mum's frown disappeared and she gave a little laugh of relief. 'I can see what the matter is, Bobby,' she said. 'You've gone and put your shoes on the wrong feet. No wonder your feet are hurting you.'

The minute Bobby took off his shoes, the pain stopped. He put them back on, this time on the feet they were meant for and everything was now fine. His feet no longer were sore and he could walk properly.

It's always uncomfortable and sometimes it's painful to be wearing something that doesn't fit. It can be like that, for instance, if we wear someone else's clothes. It's like that, too, with Christian faith. It's no good wearing someone else's. We need to have our own.